Fearfully and Wonderfully Made

By: Sharonda Williams Engram

Illustrator: Guy Wolek

XULON PRESS

Xulon Press
2301 Lucien Way #415
Maitland, FL 32751
407.339.4217
www.xulonpress.com

© 2020 by By Sharonda Williams Engram
Illustrations by Guy Wolek

All rights reserved solely by the author. The author guarantees all contents are original and do not infringe upon the legal rights of any other person or work. No part of this book may be reproduced in any form without the permission of the author. The views expressed in this book are not necessarily those of the publisher.

Unless otherwise indicated, Scripture quotations taken from the King James Version (KJV)–*public domain*.

Printed in the United States of America.

Paperback ISBN-13: 9781632213785
Hard Cover ISBN-13: 9781632213792
Ebook ISBN-13: 9781632213808

This book is dedicated to my sons of power and greatness. **Christion, Langston, Jonathon, and Justus Engram.** Daddy and mommy love you very much and we are so **blessed by our Lord and Savior, Jesus Christ,** for blessing us with you. You all are **the gift** God has **blessed** and a precious inheritance to us. It is because of you guys **this book** was discovered and developed. And to my husband, **Omari A. Engram**, for all your **love and support** in making this book **become a reality for our family.**

Fearfully in the Hebrew language is "**Yare**".
It means "to be **afraid, standing in awe, fear**."
In Psalms 139:14,
fearfully means to **stand in awe**.

Fearfully also means **reverence, honor, respect,** to case astonishment **and awe,** be held in awe, **and awesome**.
(Strong's Concordance #3372)

Fearfully and Wonderfully Made

Do you know that God knew you and gave you a **purpose** before you were in **your mommy's belly**?

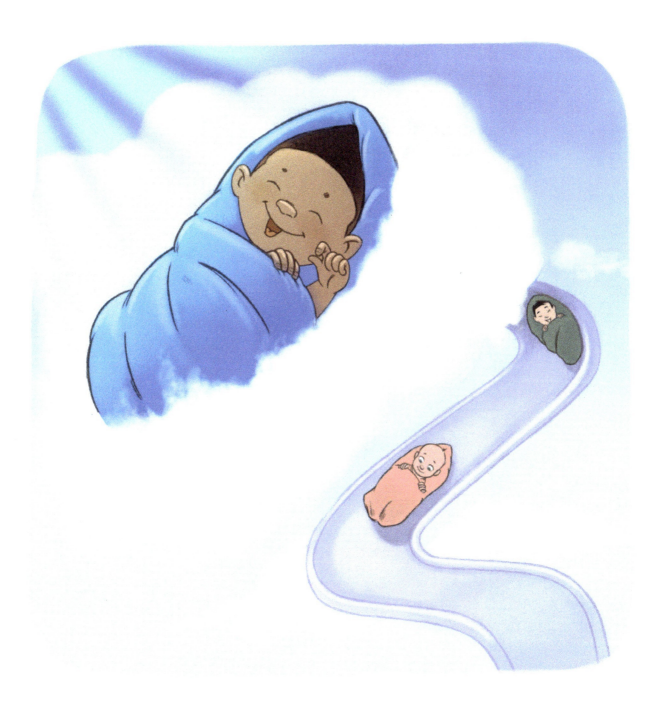

Jeremiah 1:5

Do you know that while you were in your **mommy's** tummy, **God was watching** over you day and night?

Psalm 139:16

Fearfully and Wonderfully Made

Before your **mommy and daddy** met you, you were in the heart and mind of **God**. He blessed your parents with you as a **gift from Him**.

Say, "I am a child of God!"
Psalm 127:3

He knows the number of **hairs** that you have on **your head**.

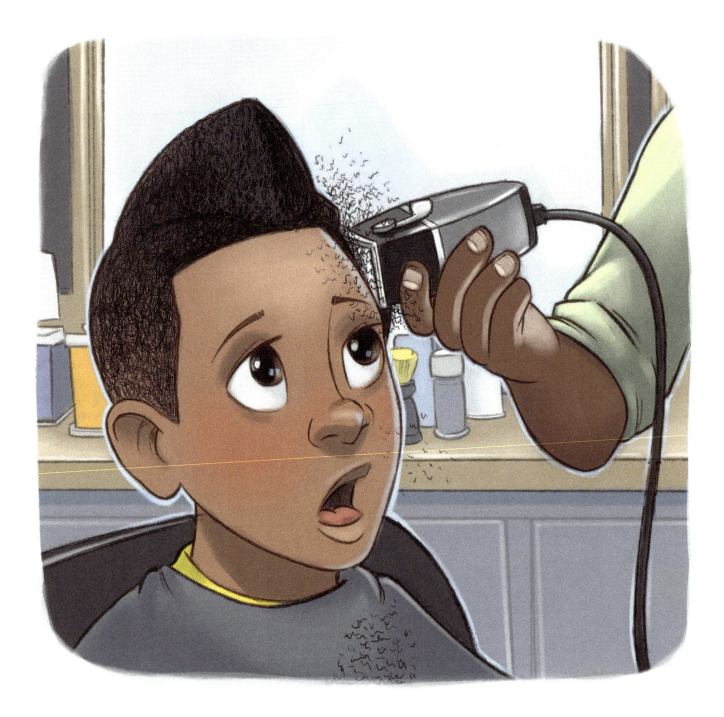

Luke 12:7

God loves you so much, that He gave **His only son**, Jesus, to have you in **His family**.

— John 3:16 —

He says you are **fearfully** and **wonderfully** made!

Psalm 139:14

God say's when **He made you**,
He was in **awe** of His beautiful creation, **you!**
You are his **masterpiece**. God respects and honors you.
You are an **inheritance** from Him.

Say, "I am fearfully and wonderfully made!"

— **Psalm 127:3.** —

He **made you to look** just like Him in the way you **talk**, **behave**, and **treat** others. You are perfectly designed!

Say, "I am made in the likeness of God!"

Genesis 1:26

When God lives **on the inside of us**, we are **everything He is**, and we can do **everything He can do**.

=== I John 4:17 ===

He guides us on how to live by His fruits.

What are **His fruits**? Love, joy, **peace**, patience, kindness, **goodness**, faithfulness, gentleness, and **self-control**. These fruits brings out your **good character** and love for God.

Galatians 5:22

God is love, so are you. His love **does not** make us afraid. It makes us **strong, confident, and bold**.

Say, "I am love!"

I John 4:8

Fearfully and Wonderfully Made

God called you **great** when you were **a thought in His mind**. Why? Because you **are from Him** and He is great. Jesus was called **great** before His daddy and mommy met Him, and He came into the world and **did great things**.

Luke 1:32

Fearfully and Wonderfully Made

Did you know Jesus was a great carpenter? He and His father, Joseph, made the best furniture. You can be a great doctor, lawyer, judge, skilled dancer, athlete; teacher, astronaut, scientist, musician, pastor, President of the USA, or business owner; all for the kingdom of God.

Mark 6:3

Fearfully and Wonderfully Made

Can you **believe and receive** your greatness?

Say, "I am great!"
══ 1 John 4:4 ══

Jesus obeyed His daddy, mommy, teachers, and laws of His land. One day at the age of 12, His **daddy and mommy** could not find Him, He walked away from His daddy and mommy to talk with the **priest** about the Holy Scriptures.

Luke 2:46

When **His parents** found Him, they instructed Him to **come and follow** them, and He was **obedient** and followed them **back home**.

Luke 2:51

Jesus **is obedient**, and He lives **in us**. We are to be **obedient** to our daddy, mommy, teachers, and **laws of our land**.

Say, "**I am obedient!**"

Ephesians 6:1

When you **obey** God, it **pleases Him**. As you grow up and grow in **knowing God**, His voice will become **clear to you**, so you can follow the paths **He leads** you to.

Proverbs 3:5-6

Because Jesus **grew up** in God and He lives on the **inside of us**, we grow up.

Say, "I grow up in God!"
― Luke 2:52 ―

God **always wants us** to tell the truth and to follow the truth. **Being truthful keeps us** close to God. **Lying** is of **darkness** and it causes us to **move away** from God. He gives us power to be **holy like Him**, so you do not have to try to be holy by yourself. **God is with you**.

Say, "**I am holy!**"

Ephesians 1:4 John 14:6

God said when we receive the Holy Spirit, we will be able to be His witness to show people His love in all the earth. The Holy Spirit was with Jesus and He is with you.

Say, "The Holy Spirit is with me!"

Acts 1:8

God gave us **all our emotions** and He has a way that we **work through them**. He said it is okay to be **angry**, but do not **sin**. It's okay to feel sad, mad, or become angry; **but do not do anything** to hurt yourself or others when you are **upset**.

Psalms 4:4-5

Fearfully and Wonderfully Made

Do not call yourself **ugly names** or anyone else names when you **feel down**. God does not want you **to hit others** because you are **upset** or break other's **belongings**. This is **not Gods way** and best for you.

Luke 10:27

God says, when you become **angry**, to sit on your bed to calm down, then come back with a **good attitude**.

Say, "I am taking charge of my emotions!"

Psalm 4:4-5

Fearfully and Wonderfully Made

Every day is a day of **thanksgiving**. Why? Because **God gives us** another day to see **His beautiful creation** and to live in **His purpose**. Jesus was thankful to His Father every day for **everything**.

Matthew 11:25

Because Jesus **lives in us**, and He is thankful, we are to have a **heart of thanksgiving**.

Say, "**I am thankful!**"

Mark 8:6

We are made with **a heart to give daily**. We can give kind words, **friendship**, hugs, **laughter**, a helping hand, **an ear to listen**, a pencil, **a sheet of paper**, share a lunch, or **give money** to help God's word go around the **world**.

II Corinthians 9:7-8

No matter how big or small, you are blessed to be a blessing to others.

Say, "I am a giver!"

John 3:16

In **everything** that we do, it is **important** that we talk to God daily. **This is called prayer**. He loves to hear from us. In **talking** to Him daily, **we grow strong** in knowing Him. He **knows us** all so well. He loves to hear **our love** for Him and our heart of **thankfulness**.

Say, "I am a leader in prayer!"
Matthew 6:9-13

You are **never too young** to follow the ways of God. God said, "even a child is **known by his doings**, whether his work is **pure**, and whether it be **right**."

Proverbs 20:11

In **everything** you do, **God** is with you. He **promised** that He will **never leave you** or forget you.

Deuteronomy 31:6

For it **pleased God** to call you to do **something great**.

You Are Awesome!

Jeremiah 1:10

Prayer to Salvation

If you read this book and just met Jesus for the first time and would like to invite Him in your heart. Here is a prayer you can pray to welcome Him in your life. Say,

Jesus I believe you are the son of God and you came to give me a long life. Thank you, Jesus, for what you did for me on the cross. I receive you into my heart today As my Savior and Lord. I choose today to live for you.

If you prayed this prayer, you have been saved.

This is an Awesome Day for You!
Go forth and be fruitful!

Scriptures for Kids

to see how IMPORTANT they are to Jesus

- **Genesis 1:26-28** – You are made in the image and of the likeness of God.
- **Psalms 27:10-14** – When you parents leave you, God will take care of you.
- **Psalms 82:6** – You are children of the Most High God.
- **Proverbs 14:26** – God is your refuge.
- **Mark 10:13-14** – Jesus told disciples to allow the children to come to Him.
- **John 10:10** – The devil come to steal, kill, and destroy, but Jesus comes that you might have life.
- **John 10:28** – No one can take you out of the hands of God.
- **Romans 10:9** – If you say you believe in Jesus with all your heart, you can be saved.
- **Romans 10:13** – If you call on Jesus name, you will be saved.
- **2 Corinthians 5:17** – You are a new creature in Christ.
- **Philippians 4:13** – You can do all things through Christ which strengthens you.
- **1 John 4:4** – You are of God.

V·i·s·i·t
Fearfully and Wonderfully Made
website at
www.madeinhisimage4.com

to download music and learn about new updates

Thank You!

CPSIA information can be obtained
at www.ICGtesting.com
Printed in the USA
BVHW022206031120
592486BV00006B/23